GENEVA, TRAVEL GUIDE 2023

Discover Switzerland's Charm

| 5-Star Hotels, Lake Cruises,

Local Delicacies, and More!"

Angelia J. Rea

Table Of Contents

INTRODUCTION

Welcome to Geneva

 Chloe has always been charmed by Geneva's allure and beauty. She had heard tales about this enchanted city perched on the shores of Lake Geneva as a young child growing up in a tiny village. Her aspirations of one day discovering its delights were kindled by tales of its rich history, beautiful scenery, and vibrant culture.

Chloe now had a rush of anticipation and excitement as she stood in the center of the metropolis. The magnificent structures lining the cobblestone streets gave off a timeless beauty. She was in awe of the magnificent structures all about her, from the Jet d'Eau, which cast a shimmering spray against the snow-capped Alps, to the splendor of St. Pierre Cathedral, which towered over her with its Gothic spires.

Chloe continued exploring and found the city to have a thriving multicultural vibe. She was tempted to immerse herself in the local culture by the bustling cafes and shops. She took a stroll along Lake Geneva's shoreline, where the calm waters mirrored the beauty of the surroundings. With its vibrant flowerbeds and renowned L'Horloge Fleurie (flower clock), the Jardin Anglais served as a tranquil haven in the middle of the busy metropolis.

In the Old Town, Chloe's explorations led her to wander through winding lanes and find hidden treasures at every turn. She marveled by the fine intricacies of the Maison de Rousseau, where the famed philosopher Jean-Jacques Rousseau once resided, as well as the Maison Tavel, the oldest house in Geneva.

Chloe immersed herself in the cultural offers of the city, exploring the rich history of Geneva at renowned museums like the Musée d'Art et d'Histoire and the Red Cross Museum. She saw the city's enthusiasm for the arts come to life while attending concerts at the Grand Théâtre.

Chloe was drawn to the area for many reasons than just its attractive appearance and diverse culture. She discovered Genevans to be friendly, hospitable, and wonderfully diversified. She bonded with locals and other travelers with ease, making new acquaintances along the way.

As Chloe's time in Geneva came to an end, she left behind cherished memories of a place that had surpassed all of her expectations. In addition to exceeding her expectations, Geneva inspired a lifelong passion for travel, culture, and the seemingly limitless opportunities that lie beyond her city. She was aware that her voyage had only just begun, and she was looking forward to the subsequent events.

CHAPTER 1 : BRIEF HISTORY

 The events that have woven together in Geneva's history to create the amazing city it is today have moulded the city's identity. Since ancient times, Geneva's strategic location on the beaches of Lake Geneva has made it a significant crossroads for trade and travel. It is located at the westernmost point of Switzerland. It is possible to trace the city's history back to the Roman era, when it was known as "Genava." Geneva was an important trading centre and a stopping point for travellers crossing the Alps under the Roman Empire.

Geneva's fate was intertwined with that of the dominant House of Savoy, who dominated the area, during the Middle Ages. The Protestant

Reformation, however, was a key turning point in the city's history in the 16th century and altered its course irrevocably. Geneva served as a major location for the spread of Protestantism under the sway of John Calvin. As the "Protestant Rome," the city embraced its reputation for drawing intellectuals, reformers, and Protestant exiles from all across Europe.

Geneva became a sovereign republic in 1536 after gaining independence from the House of Savoy amid religious strife and shifting alliances. The inhabitants of the city accepted a distinctive form of government, nurturing a spirit of liberty, tolerance, and human rights that has since come to characterise Geneva.

In the 19th century, Geneva started to gain a reputation as a hub of international diplomacy and humanitarianism. An important turning point in Geneva's dedication to humanitarian ideals was the founding of the International Committee of the Red Cross in 1863.

The city became a significant global centre for international organisations during the 20th century. From 1920 to 1946, the League of Nations, the forerunner of the United Nations, had its headquarters in Geneva. Geneva's status as a hub of diplomacy and international cooperation was cemented after World War II when it was chosen to serve as the United Nations' regional headquarters in Europe. Geneva is known for its dedication to world peace, human rights, and international collaboration. It is a modern, multicultural city. Its attraction is increased by the gorgeous surroundings, which feature Lake Geneva in the foreground and the Alps in the distance. Geneva continues to play a crucial role in determining the path of world affairs as a melting pot of cultures and a hub for diplomacy. It also stands as a ray of hope for a more peaceful and just world.

The Top Twenty Reasons To Visit Geneva

1. Discover Geneva's rich history, which spans from its Roman origins to its participation in the Protestant Reformation and its status as a centre of international diplomacy.

2. **Beautiful Lake Geneva**: Take in the breathtaking views of the lake as it is encircled by the towering Alps, and partake in water sports like boating and swimming or just unwind on the lakeside promenades.

3. **Cultural Wonders**: Get lost in Geneva's thriving cultural scene, where top-notch galleries, theatres, concerts, and museums provide a wide variety of artistic experiences.

4. **Old Town Charm**: Get lost in Geneva's Old Town's winding lanes while

admiring the mediaeval buildings, touring ancient sites like St. Pierre Cathedral, and finding hidden treasures around every bend.

5. **As the European headquarters of the United Nations** and the home to numerous international institutions and embassies, the city is a hub for diplomacy on a global scale.

6. Learn about Geneva's enormous contribution to humanitarian operations, including the creation of the International Red Cross and Red Crescent Movement, in this section on the city's humanitarian legacy.

7. **Multicultural Cuisine**: Geneva's culinary scene, which offers a wide variety of international cuisines, from gourmet Michelin-starred restaurants to Swiss delicacies, will delight your taste buds.

8. Explore the city's upscale shops and luxury stores, especially those along the renowned Rue du Rhône, which provide a lovely shopping experience for fashion fans.

9. Discover the surrounding natural splendour at nature retreats, where you can go hiking, skiing, and engaging in other outdoor activities in the Jura and Alps mountains nearby.

10. Attend the famed Geneva International Motor Show to see the newest technologies and high-end vehicles, which draws auto aficionados from all over the world.

11. Discover the fascinating world of Swiss watchmaking with visits to illustrious watch museums and opulent watch shops that highlight the city's horological heritage. This is the tradition of watchmaking in Geneva.

12. Wine tastings and spectacular views of the sprawling vineyards may be had by making a quick trip to the picturesque vineyards in the Lake Geneva area.

13. Admire the famous L'Horloge Fleurie (flower clock), a representation of Geneva's commitment to accuracy and horticulture, which is housed in the lovely Jardin Anglais.

14. **Jet d'Eau**: At the shore of Lake Geneva, you'll find the renowned Jet d'Eau, an astonishing water fountain that rises almost 450 feet into the air.

15. **International Film Festival**: Attend the Geneva International Film Festival to celebrate world cinema and to have the chance to speak with renowned directors.

16. Discover the bohemian neighbourhood of Carouge, which is renowned for its quaint squares, artisan shops, and exciting nightlife.

17. Visit the European Organisation for Nuclear Research (CERN) to see the cutting-edge research being done at the biggest particle physics facility in the world.

18. Enjoy some of the world-famous Swiss chocolate while in Geneva, which is home to a number of renowned chocolatiers and offers chocolate sampling excursions.

19. The highest peak in the Alps, the spectacular Mont Blanc, can be seen from Chamonix, France, where you can also go skiing, hiking, or take a cable car ride.

20. **Festivals in Geneva**: Take part in the fun at Geneva's yearly events, such the Fêtes de Genève, a bustling summer festival with fireworks, concerts, and cultural acts.

The Best Way To Get There

Since Geneva has a well-connected transportation system, getting there is not too difficult. Some of the finest ways to go to this lovely city are listed below:

- **By Air**: A significant hub for international flights, Geneva International Airport is conveniently close to the city centre. It is convenient for travellers from all over the world because it provides direct connections to many cities throughout the world.

- **By Train**: Major Swiss cities and neighbouring nations have strong links to Geneva thanks to Switzerland's effective rail network. Because of the city's direct train connections to places like Zurich, Basel, Lausanne, and even Paris, taking the train is a relaxing and beautiful alternative.

- **By Car**: With well-maintained roadways linking it to the rest of Switzerland and its neighbours, Geneva is easily reachable by car. The Swiss countryside is beautiful, and driving through it can be a pleasant experience thanks to the superb road infrastructure.

- **By Bus**: Geneva is connected to numerous cities and towns around Europe and Switzerland by a vast bus network. For those on a tight budget, long-distance bus operators provide economical solutions.

- **By Boat**: Geneva can be reached by boat via Lake Geneva for an unusual and picturesque route. Ferry services connect the Swiss communities along the lake, and the trip is scenic.

Once in Geneva, it is simple to go around and experience the city and its surrounds thanks to the effective public transit system in the city, which includes buses, trams, and trains. Geneva is a pedestrian-friendly city thanks to its small size, which lets visitors explore many sights on foot.

Getting Around Geneva

- **Trams**: The vast tram network in Geneva connects the city centre to its periphery. With frequent service and routes connecting important attractions, neighbourhoods, and transportation hubs, trams are a well-liked and practical method of transportation.

- **Buses**: Geneva's bus system provides supplementary coverage for places that the tram system does not reach. Buses operate on a detailed timetable and provide flexibility for seeing the city's various neighbourhoods thanks to their numerous routes.

- **Trains**: Geneva is connected to other Swiss towns as well as nearby countries by the effective train network run by the Swiss Federal Railways (SBB). Train travel is a fantastic way to explore the beautiful Swiss countryside or go on day getaways.

- **Boats**: With its boat services, Lake Geneva provides a distinctive means of transportation. Take in the scenery as you ride to numerous lakeside villages and cities, including well-known locations like Montreux and Lausanne.

- **Cycling**: Geneva is a bike-friendly city with well marked bike lanes and a bike-sharing programme known as "Genève Roule." Especially in the warmer months, renting a bicycle is a terrific way to tour the city at your own pace.

- **Walking**: Geneva is a great city for walking because of its small size and thoughtful planning. The Old Town, the lakeside promenades, and commercial districts are just a few of the sights that are conveniently reachable by foot.
- Taxis and ride-sharing services are readily available across the city, and Uber and other ride-sharing services are available in Geneva.

Additionally, Geneva provides free access to public transportation for the duration of a visitor's stay with the "Geneva Transport Card" for those staying in hotels.

Getting around Geneva is simple and effective because to its great transit system and range of options, allowing visitors to easily enjoy the city's attractions, cultural landmarks, and natural beauty.

CHAPTER 2: ARE YOU PLANNING A TRIP TO GENEVA?

What To Bring Along On Your Trip

- **Travel Documents**: Bring your passport, identification, and any visas or travel permits you may require. It's also a good idea to preserve duplicates of these documents in case of an emergency.

- **Clothing for the Weather**: Geneva has four distinct seasons, so pack clothing appropriate for the weather during your visit. Bring layers because temperatures can fluctuate throughout the day. Pack lightweight and breathable clothing in the summer, and warm gear in the winter, including a coat, hat, gloves, and scarves.

- **Comfortable Shoes**: Because Geneva is a walkable city, comfortable shoes are essential. Pack a pair of sturdy walking shoes or sneakers to easily explore the city's cobblestone streets and sights.

- **Adapters and chargers**: Switzerland utilises the normal European two-pin plug, so pack a universal adaptor if you want to charge your electronic gadgets. Remember to bring chargers for your phone, camera, and other electronic devices.

- Carry a travel guide or download a reputable travel app to help you navigate the city. When touring Geneva's streets, maps or a GPS system can come in handy.

- **Language Translation Apps and Pocket Dictionaries**: Although English is widely spoken in Geneva, owning a language translation app or pocket dictionary can help you communicate with locals or read signs.

- **Drugs and First Aid Kit**: If you need to take prescription drugs, make sure you bring enough for the duration of your trip. It's also a good idea to bring a basic first-aid kit with items like band-aids, pain medicines, and any personal medication you might need.

- **Travel Insurance**: Having travel insurance that covers medical emergencies, trip cancellations, and loss of belongings is essential. Carry the appropriate documentation and contact information with you in case of an emergency.

- **Money and Credit Cards**: Have some Swiss Francs (CHF) in cash on hand for little purchases or establishments that may not accept credit cards. It is also advisable to bring a credit or debit card for larger purchases or emergencies.

- A tiny daypack or bag is ideal for transporting items on day trips or sightseeing excursions.

Remember to check the weather forecast before your trip so you can prepare appropriately, and leave some room in your suitcase for any souvenirs or products you may purchase during your stay to Geneva.

Children And Geneva

Geneva is a fantastic destination for families with children, with a wealth of activities and sights geared towards children. Here's why children and Geneva go together so well:

- **Parks and Playgrounds**: Geneva has a plethora of parks and playgrounds where children may run, play, and have a good time. The Parc des Bastions, with its massive chessboard and playgrounds, is a popular destination, as is the Jardin Anglais, with its merry-go-round and picnic areas.

- **Museums for Children**: There are various museums in Geneva that include parts dedicated to children. The Museum of Natural History's interactive exhibitions, the Museum of Art and History's "Museum in a Trunk" programme, and the Patek Philippe Museum's watchmaking workshops are just a few examples of fun museum experiences for kids.

- **Lake Activities**: The calm waters of Lake Geneva provide a variety of family-friendly activities. Take a boat trip, rent paddleboats, or simply relax with a lakeside lunch while admiring the surroundings.

- **Animal Parks and Zoos**: Children will enjoy visiting Geneva's animal parks and zoos. Popular options include the Parc Animalier Pierre Challandes and the Zoo La Garenne, which provide close interactions with a range of animals as well as educational programmes.

- **Adventure Parks**: For a thrill, Geneva boasts adventure parks that offer thrilling experiences for children. Zip lines, climbing walls, and obstacle courses are available in Forestland and Vitam'Parc Adventure Park to keep kids entertained and active.

- **Festivals and Events**: Throughout the year, Geneva holds a variety of family-friendly festivals and events. The Escalade Festival, Geneva's Christmas Market, and the Fêtes de Genève are just a few examples of festivals that provide youngsters with entertainment and activities.

- **Swiss Chocolate & delights**: Switzerland is well-known for its delectable chocolate, and Geneva offers numerous opportunities to indulge in sweet delights. Children will have a great time touring chocolate stores, engaging in chocolate workshops, and sampling the exquisite Swiss confections.

Geneva is an outstanding family vacation due to its safe and child-friendly atmosphere. The city's commitment to delivering engaging experiences for children guarantees that youngsters have a memorable and pleasurable vacation.

Geneva's Nightlife Is Exciting.

 When the sun goes down, Geneva comes alive, providing inhabitants and visitors with a unique nightlife experience.

The bustling bar scene is one of the highlights of Geneva's nightlife. There is a place for every mood, from contemporary rooftop bars with amazing views of Lake Geneva to cosy pubs tucked away in quaint neighbourhoods. Whether you're looking for craft cocktails, premium wines, or locally brewed beers, the city's bars have something for everyone. These venues frequently hold live music performances, DJ sets, and themed evenings, resulting in a dynamic atmosphere that keeps the party going into the early hours of the morning.

Geneva has a handful of upmarket nightclubs for people looking for a more upscale experience. These venues have top-notch sound systems, internationally famous DJs, and trendy décor, providing a glamorous and exciting atmosphere. High-end clubs in the city attract a diverse and sophisticated population, ensuring a fantastic night out.

Geneva also has a robust performing arts scene. Several theatres and concert venues in the city feature a wide range of acts, including classical music concerts, ballets, operas, and theatrical shows. Whether you prefer classical music or contemporary shows, there are plenty of opportunities to enjoy the arts in the evening.

Furthermore, Geneva has a variety of entertainment opportunities in addition to the conventional nightlife locations. The city frequently hosts cultural events, art exhibitions, and nighttime festivals. There's usually something going on in Geneva after dark, from open-air concerts and street performances to art installations and food festivals.

Culture And People

The cultural scene in Geneva is active and diverse. Numerous museums, art galleries, and cultural organisations in the city present a diverse spectrum of artistic expressions. For example, the Museum of paintings and History has a large collection of paintings from many periods, and the Museum of Natural History has fascinating exhibits on the region's flora, wildlife, and geology. Furthermore, the Contemporary Art Centre and the Fondation Baur present contemporary and Asian art, respectively, broadening the cultural offers.

Genevans, often known as "Genevois," are noted for their cosmopolitanism and open-mindedness. The city attracts people from all over the world, including diplomats, international business executives, and researchers, which contributes to its multiculturalism. As a result, Geneva has become a cultural, linguistic, and traditional melting pot. It is not uncommon to hear a variety of languages spoken on the streets, reflecting the cosmopolitan character of the city. The population of Geneva is distinguished by a high level of education and a strong emphasis on knowledge and creativity. Numerous scientific organisations, including CERN (the European Organisation for Nuclear scientific), attract scientists and researchers from all over the world. This intellectual environment nurtures a spirit of curiosity, invention, and dedication to knowledge advancement.

Another distinguishing feature of Geneva's culture is its regard for humanitarian principles and its status as an international diplomatic centre. As the European headquarters of the United Nations and other international organisations, the city serves as a hub for global collaboration and dialogue. The existence of the International Red Cross and Red Crescent Museum, which honours the efforts of both organisations, exemplifies Geneva's devotion to human rights and humanitarian issues.

Discounts And Information On Sightseeing Passes

Geneva is a lovely city with much to offer visitors. Geneva has something for everyone, from its famed Jet d'Eau fountain to its world-renowned institutions. If you're going to Geneva, you should think about getting a sightseeing permit.

The Geneva City Pass and the Swiss Travel Pass are the two main sightseeing passes offered in Geneva.

The City Pass for Geneva

The Geneva City Pass is an excellent choice for travellers who wish to experience the best that

Geneva has to offer. The card grants free admission to more than 40 attractions, including the Musée d'Art et d'Histoire, the Natural History Museum, and the United Nations Headquarters. The pass also offers free Geneva public transit and discounts on a variety of other activities.

The Geneva City Pass can be purchased for 24, 48, or 72 hours. The following are the prices:

24 hours: CHF 20.80

48 hours: CHF 29.80

72 hours: CHF 36.00

Switzerland Travel Pass

The Swiss Travel Pass is a more comprehensive pass that is valid on all Swiss public transit. The card also grants free admission to over 500 museums and attractions.

The Swiss Travel Pass is offered for three, four, eight, or fifteen days. The following are the prices:

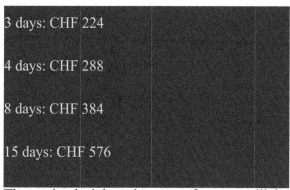

3 days: CHF 224

4 days: CHF 288

8 days: CHF 384

15 days: CHF 576

The optimal sightseeing pass for you will be determined by your specific needs and interests. The Geneva City Pass is an excellent alternative if you only want to explore the key attractions in Geneva. If you intend to travel extensively throughout Switzerland, the Swiss Travel Pass is a better option.

Whatever pass you choose, you will have a fantastic day visiting Geneva.

CHAPTER 3: GENEVA ACCOMMODATION

Tips For Locating And Reserving Lodging

Here are some pointers to help you choose and book the ideal Geneva accommodation:

- **Begin early**: Because Geneva is a popular tourist location, it's critical to start your search early in order to secure the best selections at competitive pricing.

- **Establish your budget**: Set a firm budget for your lodging to help you narrow down your options. Geneva has a variety of lodging alternatives, ranging from luxury hotels to low-cost hostels.

- **Investigate several neighbourhoods**: Geneva has distinct neighbourhoods, each with its own ambiance and amenities. Take into account your tastes and priorities, such as closeness to attractions, public transit, or a peaceful environment.

- **Use online platforms**: Websites and apps like as Booking.com, Airbnb, and Expedia provide a diverse range of rooms in Geneva. Read customer reviews, compare pricing, and look for any hidden fees or policies.

- **Consider the following alternatives**: Aside from standard hotels, consider vacation rentals, serviced apartments, or bed & breakfasts. These can deliver a more personalised experience and are frequently more cost effective.

- **Contact the lodging directly**: If you have unique demands or questions, contact the lodging directly to verify they can accommodate them.

- Consider the amenities you want, such as free Wi-Fi, breakfast, parking, or a fitness centre. Check that the accommodation you've chosen has the amenities you'll need to enjoy your stay.

- Read the cancellation terms carefully before making a reservation to prevent any surprises or charges if your plans change.

Recommendations For Various Budget Levels When Visiting

To assist you maximise your trip without going over budget, the following suggestions are provided:

- **Attractions that are affordable**: Geneva has a number of free or inexpensive attractions. Discover the charming Old Town, go to St. Pierre Cathedral, wander along the promenades along Lake Geneva, and take in the lovely parks and gardens.

- Use Geneva's effective public transit system, which includes buses, trams, and trains. Think about getting a Geneva Transport Card, which provides limitless travel throughout the city for a predetermined amount of time and is frequently offered free of charge by your lodging.
- **Affordable dining options**: For tasty meals, visit your neighbourhood cafés, bakeries, and food markets. Without going overboard, you can enjoy delectable Swiss specialties like cheese fondue and raclette.
- Take advantage of the breathtaking Lake Geneva surroundings and have a picnic there. To purchase fresh produce, cheese, and bread, visit neighbourhood markets like Plainpalais Market or Bastions Market.

- **Free museum days**: On certain days or at specific times, many museums in Geneva are free to enter. Plan your trip appropriately to enjoy museums like the Museum of Art and History, Patek Philippe Museum, or Maison Tavel without breaking the bank.

- **Options for lodging**: Take into consideration staying in hostels, guesthouses, or low-cost hotels. Through websites like Airbnb, you may also look at holiday rentals or shared lodgings.

- Check out the Geneva Pass or other discount cards, which provide reduced or free admission to a variety of sites, access to public transportation, and other benefits.

- **Utilise the environment**: Geneva is surrounded by breathtaking natural beauty. Swim in the lake, go trekking on local trails, or just take in the spectacular views of the Swiss Alps.

5 Expensive Hotels to Stay at While Visiting

Geneva's Ritz-Carlton Hotel de la Paix

Prices: start at CHF 1,500 per night.

Amenities: include a five-star hotel with opulent rooms, excellent dining restaurants, a spa, and a fitness centre.

The hotel is located in the centre of Geneva, near the lake and the UN Headquarters.

Highlights: The hotel dates back to 1865 and has a long and illustrious history. Over the years, it has welcomed many renowned guests, including Queen Elizabeth II and Grace Kelly.

Geneva's President Wilson Hotel

Prices: start at CHF 1,200 per night.

A 5-star hotel with breathtaking views of Lake Geneva, a Michelin-starred restaurant, a spa, and a fitness centre are among the amenities.

Location: On the shores of Lake Geneva, with panoramic views of the Alps.

Highlights: include the hotel's rooftop terrace, which offers panoramic views of the city and the lake. There is also a private beach club.

Geneva Four Seasons Hotel des Bergues

Prices: start at CHF 1,100 per night.

A 5-star hotel with exquisite rooms, a Michelin-starred restaurant, a spa, and a fitness centre are among the amenities.

The hotel is located in the middle of Geneva, near the lake and the commercial district.

The hotel offers a stunning lobby with a big staircase. It also boasts a rooftop terrace with city and lake views.

Geneva's Mandarin Oriental

Prices start at CHF 1,000 per night.

A 5-star hotel with magnificent rooms, a Michelin-starred restaurant, a spa, and a fitness centre are among the amenities.

The hotel is located in the middle of Geneva, near the lake and the commercial district.

Highlights include the hotel's exquisite spa, which has a hammam and a sauna. It also boasts a rooftop terrace with city and lake views.

Geneva Beau-Rivage

Prices start at CHF 900 per night.

A 5-star hotel with exquisite rooms, a Michelin-starred restaurant, a spa, and a fitness centre are among the amenities.

Location: On the shores of Lake Geneva, with panoramic views of the Alps.

The hotel features a lovely garden with a patio facing the lake. There is also a private beach club.

5 low-cost hotels to stay in when visiting

The Alpes Hotel

Prices start at CHF 100 per night.

Amenities include a clean room, a bar, and a breakfast buffet.

The hotel is located in the middle of Geneva, near the lake and the train station.

Highlights: The motel is reasonably priced and conveniently placed. It is an excellent choice for budget travellers.

Geneva Youth Hostel

Price: A dorm bed starts at CHF 40 per night.

Hostel facilities include shared dorms, individual rooms, a kitchen, and a laundry facility.

The hotel is located in the middle of Geneva, near the lake and the train station.

Highlights: The hostel has a terrific environment and is highly friendly. It is an excellent choice for backpackers and budget travellers.

Hotel City Hostel Geneva in Geneva

Price: A dorm bed starts at CHF 50 per night.

Hostel facilities include shared dorms, individual rooms, a kitchen, and a laundry facility.

The hotel is located in the middle of Geneva, near the lake and the train station.

Highlights: The hostel has a terrific environment and is highly friendly. It is an excellent choice for backpackers and budget travellers.

Budget Ibis Geneva Centre Gare

Prices start at CHF 80 per night.

Amenities include a clean room, a bar, and a breakfast buffet.

The hotel is located in the middle of Geneva, near the train station and the lake.

Highlights: The motel is reasonably priced and conveniently placed. It is an excellent choice for budget travellers.

THE B&B HOTEL Geneva International Airport

Prices start at CHF 60 per night.

Amenities include a clean room, a bar, and a breakfast buffet.

The hotel is close to the airport and has convenient access to public transit.

Highlights: The motel is reasonably priced and conveniently located. It is an excellent choice for budget travellers travelling into Geneva.

CHAPTER 4: GENEVA DINING AND DRINKING

A Look At The Culinary Scene

This cosmopolitan city offers a delectable blend of traditional Swiss cuisine and a wide range of international flavours, making it a foodie's heaven.

One cannot visit Geneva's culinary scene without mentioning its famous cheese fondue. Melted cheese, mainly Gruyère and Emmental, is blended with white wine and garlic and served with bits of bread for dipping. Many Geneva restaurants specialise in this delectable delicacy, with various variants to suit every palate.

Aside from fondue, Geneva has a plethora of gourmet restaurants that demonstrate the city's dedication to culinary quality. These restaurants provide unique and polished meals that tantalise the taste buds by focusing on fresh, locally sourced ingredients. There is something to please every culinary need, from Michelin-starred restaurants to contemporary bistros.

The multinational community has a strong influence on Geneva's culinary scene. As a worldwide organisation centre and cultural melting pot, the city accepts flavours from all over the world. Whether you want Italian pasta, French patisserie, or spicy Indian curries, you'll find a variety of restaurants and cafes to suit your interests.

Furthermore, Geneva has a plethora of gourmet food markets and artisanal shops. Fresh produce, local cheeses, cured meats, and freshly baked bread are all available at the crowded farmer's markets. These markets are not only a sensory treat, but they also symbolise the city's commitment to sustainability and supporting local farmers.

For those looking for a one-of-a-kind gastronomic experience, Geneva holds a number of food festivals and events throughout the year. There is always something fascinating going on the gastronomic calendar, from the Geneva Street Food Festival, where you can indulge in scrumptious international street food, to the Escalade Festival, which celebrates the city's rich history via food and drink.

The Best Restaurants In Geneva To Visit

- **Chez Henry**: This Michelin-starred restaurant delivers traditional French fare with a contemporary touch. Main courses begin about CHF 60.

- **Le Chat Botté**: This quaint café serves classic Swiss dishes in a welcoming ambiance. Main courses begin about CHF 40.

- **Agathe's Table**: This fine-dining establishment specialises in Mediterranean food with a seasonal focus. Main courses begin about CHF 75.

- **Le FouduFromage**: This cheese lover's heaven offers a diverse selection of cheeses from throughout the world, as well as delectable cheese-based delicacies. Main courses begin about CHF 30.

- **La Pinte Vaudoise**: This classic Swiss restaurant offers hearty dishes such as fondue and raclette. Main courses begin about CHF 35.

- **La Creperie**: This traditional crêperie provides delectable crêpes and galettes cooked from scratch. Main courses begin about CHF 15.

- **Le Tunnel**: For beverages and appetisers, this vibrant pub and restaurant is a wonderful choice. Main courses begin about CHF 20.

- **La Maison Rose**: This lovely restaurant is housed in a very old structure. It serves traditional Swiss fare with a contemporary touch. Main courses begin about CHF 40.

- **Bistrot du Boeuf Rouge**: For a casual supper, this classic French bistro is a fantastic choice. Main courses begin about CHF 30.

Whatever your budget or taste, you'll find a terrific restaurant in Geneva to enjoy.

How to get inexpensive meals during your stay

- **Explore local markets**: Geneva has a number of markets where you may discover fresh produce, regional delicacies, and reasonably priced meals. Visit the Plainpalais Market or the Carouge Market to get fresh ingredients and cook your own meals for a fraction of the price of eating out.

- **Look for low-cost restaurants**: Look for smaller restaurants, cafés, and food stalls that provide low-cost menus. These enterprises frequently cater to locals and are less pricey than tourist traps. Rue de l'Ecole-de-Médecine and Rue des Etuves are well-known for their low-cost meals.

- **Choose lunch specials**: Many Geneva restaurants offer lunch specials that are fantastic value for money. Take advantage of these offers by eating your main meal during noon rather than dinner. Fixed-price menus or discounted items are common.

- **Accept ethnic cuisine**: As a multicultural city, Geneva has a varied choice of ethnic eateries. Explore international cuisines such as Middle Eastern, Asian, and African cuisines, which can provide great meals at a lower cost than typical Swiss food.

- **Use food trucks and street food**: Geneva has a vibrant food truck culture with a wide range of economical and tasty options. Look for food truck festivals or popular food trucks around town for a quick and cheap supper on the fly.

- **Consider shopping at local supermarkets** if you have access to a kitchenette or are staying in a self-catering apartment. Migros and

Coop are two popular Geneva supermarket brands where you may buy low-cost products and ready-to-eat meals.

- **Pack a picnic**: There are many wonderful parks and scenic areas in Geneva where you may have a picnic. Pick up fresh bread, cheese, and other picnic supplies at a local bakery or deli, and spend a quiet afternoon outside while saving money on meals.

Using these tactics, you can enjoy economical meals while in Geneva without sacrificing taste or quality. Remember to try out new restaurants, take advantage of lunch specials, and enjoy the city's unique culinary culture. Bon appetite!

CHAPTER 5:GENEVA SIGHTSEEING

Top 5 Geneva Events To Attend

Here are the top five Geneva events to attend, along with their associated dates:

1. **The Geneva Motor Show (March)** is regarded as one of the most significant events in the automobile industry, showcasing the newest technologies and concept cars from major manufacturers. Car lovers from all around the world converge to see cutting-edge technologies and sleek designs unveiled. The event is usually held in early to mid-March, with visitors from March 2nd to March 12th.

2. **Montreux Jazz Festival (July):** The Montreux Jazz Festival, held in adjacent Montreux, just a short distance from Geneva, is an internationally recognised music festival that has captivated audiences for over 50 years. Renowned artists from a variety of genres, including jazz, blues, and rock, perform at spectacular settings nestled along the scenic Lake Geneva. The festival lasts two weeks and usually starts in early July.

3. **Geneva International Film Festival (November):** Every year, film fans and industry experts descend on Geneva for the Geneva International Film Festival. This festival honours independent cinema by presenting a wide range of thought-provoking films, documentaries, and experimental works. The festival, which includes screenings, workshops,

and Q&A sessions, provides a unique platform for both young and experienced filmmakers. The festival usually lasts a week, starting in mid-November.

4. **Escalade (December):** Escalade is a historical commemoration of Geneva's defence against an attack in 1602. The festival includes activities such as a torchlight parade, traditional music performances, and reenactments of historical events. Visitors can sample local specialties such as the famed chocolate cauldron while dressed in mediaeval costumes. Escalade is held every year on the weekend closest to December 12th.

5. **Lake Geneva Festival (August):** The Lake Geneva Festival, a highlight of the summer season, presents a diverse programme of arts and cultural events. In picturesque sites around Lake Geneva,

visitors may enjoy open-air concerts, dance performances, theatre plays, and exhibitions. The festival creates a lively atmosphere while highlighting the region's rich creative legacy. The festival usually lasts the entire month of August, with events happening on various dates throughout the month.

These top five Geneva events provide one-of-a-kind experiences for a wide range of interests, from car fanatics and music fans to cinema geeks and history buffs. Attending any of these events allows you to immerse yourself in the vivid culture and environment of Geneva.

Geneva's Top 15 Attractions

1. **The Jet d'Eau** is a spectacular water fountain

that shoots up to 140 metres high and is one of the city's most distinctive monuments. It is a must-see sight with a breathtaking perspective of Lake Geneva.

2. Explore the lovely cobblestone streets of the Old Town, which are full with historical buildings, quaint shops, and cafes. St. Peter's Cathedral, Maison Tavel, and Maison Rousseau are must-sees.

3. **Lake Geneva**: As Western Europe's largest lake, Lake Geneva offers scenic views and a variety of recreational activities such as boating, swimming, and lakeside picnics.

4. **United Nations Office**: Pay a visit to the Palais des Nations, the United Nations' European headquarters. Learn about global diplomacy and view the Assembly

Hall and Council Chamber on a guided tour.

5. **Patek Philippe Museum**: This renowned museum delves into the world of watchmaking. Admire an incredible collection of timepieces, which includes antique watches as well as modern masterpieces.

6. **The English Garden, or Jardin Anglais**, is a lovely park along the lakefront. Take a stroll, relax on the benches, and gaze at the famous L'Horloge Fleurie (Flower Clock).

7. **International Red Cross and Red Crescent Museum**: Learn about the Red Cross' humanitarian activities through interactive displays and multimedia presentations.

8. **Museum of Natural History**: This museum explores the wonderful realm of natural history, including displays on

dinosaurs, fossils, minerals, and local fauna.

9. **Parc des Bastions**: This gorgeous park is home to the Reformation Wall, which commemorates the Protestant Reformation leaders. Play enormous chess or simply relax in the peaceful surroundings.

10. **St. Pierre Cathedral**: Climb the spires of this magnificent cathedral for beautiful views of the city and the lake. Explore the archaeological site beneath the city, which demonstrates the city's Roman origins.

11. **Explore the different art and history collections**, which include ancient artefacts, mediaeval art, European paintings, and decorative arts.

12. **Bains des Pâquis**: Enjoy swimming, sunbathing, and resting in the saunas at this popular lakeside beach. Don't miss

out on the legendary L'Île Rousseau, a little lake island.

13. **Carouge**: Dubbed the "Greenwich Village of Geneva," this bohemian neighbourhood offers a lively environment with its colourful buildings, fashionable boutiques, and bustling cafes.

14. **Museum of Modern and Contemporary Art (MAMCO):** This cutting-edge museum features works by notable artists from the twentieth and twenty-first centuries.

15. **Explore the world of ceramics and glass at the Ariana Museum**, which has a huge collection of decorative arts from Europe and Asia.

The greatest attractions in Geneva combine natural beauty, cultural legacy, and international relevance.

Geneva itinerary for 3 days

Here's a suggested itinerary to maximise your time:

Day 1:

Begin your day by paying a visit to Geneva's most famous monument, the Jet d'Eau. Take a leisurely stroll along Lake Geneva's beaches, soaking in the stunning sights. Explore the Old Town, also known as Vieille Ville, with its tiny cobblestone alleys, attractive boutiques, and historical buildings. Don't miss the St. Pierre Cathedral, where you may climb the tower for a panoramic perspective of the city. In the afternoon, take a guided tour of the United Nations Office to learn about its worldwide significance. End your day with a leisurely boat ride on Lake Geneva, observing the beautiful scenery.

Day 2:

Take a day trip to Montreux, which is only an hour by rail from Geneva. Explore the stunning Chillon Castle on the banks of Lake Geneva. Admire its mediaeval architecture and learn about its fascinating history. After that, go along the promenade, which is lined with beautiful gardens and vivid flowers. Return to Geneva in the evening and dine at a local restaurant on Swiss cuisine.

Day 3:

Begin your day by visiting the International Red Cross and Red Crescent Museum, where you may learn about these organisations' humanitarian operations. Next, visit Carouge, a trendy neighbourhood famed for its bohemian vibe, artisan boutiques, and bustling cafes. Visit the Patek Philippe Museum, which is dedicated to the art of watchmaking. Admire the complex clocks and learn about Swiss watchmaking history. Finish your day by going to the Parc des

Bastions, which houses the famed Reformation Wall and the gigantic chessboard.

Geneva itinerary for 7 days

Day 1:

Begin your vacation in Geneva by touring the lovely Old Town (Vieille Ville). Explore its small cobblestone alleyways and pay a visit to St. Peter's Cathedral, one of the city's most recognisable attractions. The cathedral's tower offers stunning views of the city and Lake Geneva. Continue to the Maison Tavel, Geneva's oldest house, which today contains a museum highlighting the city's history.

Day 2:

Take a leisurely boat trip on Lake Geneva and take in the breathtaking scenery. Visit the famed Jet d'Eau water fountain, which shoots water up to 140 metres high. Discover the Jardin Anglais, a magnificent park with beautiful flowerbeds and the famed L'Horloge Fleurie, a clock constructed entirely of flowers.

Day 3:

Visit the United Nations Office and the Red Cross Museum to learn about Geneva's international aspect. Explore these key institutions to learn about global diplomacy and humanitarian activities.

Day 4:

Take a day trip to the adjacent picturesque French town of Annecy. Annecy, known as the "Venice of the Alps," has magnificent canals, a mediaeval castle, and a beautiful lake. Enjoy a leisurely stroll along the canals while dining on delectable French cuisine.

Day 5:

Spend the day discovering Geneva's cultural side. The Museum of Art and History houses a large collection of European art and archaeology. The Reformation Wall, a monument honouring major figures in the Protestant Reformation, should not be missed.

Day 6:

Visit the neighbouring Alps to escape to the tranquil splendour of the Swiss countryside. Travel via picturesque train to Chamonix-Mont-Blanc, a well-known mountain resort town. Enjoy stunning views of Mont Blanc, the tallest peak in the Alps, and participate in outdoor sports such as hiking or skiing.

Day 7:

Finish your Geneva schedule with some luxury shopping on Rue du Rhône, which is famed for its high-end boutiques and prestigious watchmakers. Take a quiet walk along the lakeside promenade to savour the last moments of your stay in this lovely city.

CHAPTER 6: GENEVA SHOPPING

Overview Of The Geneva Shopping Scene

 The Geneva shopping scene is a treat for both locals and visitors alike. This dynamic city in Switzerland is known as one of the world's best shopping destinations, catering to a wide range of tastes and budgets. Geneva has something for everyone, from fancy boutiques to charming marketplaces.

The Rue du Rhône is the city's most prominent retail district, home to renowned worldwide companies like as Chanel, Louis Vuitton, and

Rolex. Shoppers can treat themselves to fine couture, high-end accessories, and magnificent jewellery. Nearby, the picturesque Old Town offers a unique shopping experience, with tiny alleys lined with individual shops and antique stores, ideal for those looking for one-of-a-kind bargains and mementos.

The Plainpalais flea market is a must-see for a sample of local culture. It is held on Wednesdays and Saturdays and features a treasure trove of antique clothing, books, and collectibles. The Carouge district, which is influenced by Italian architecture, has a bohemian vibe and is noted for its artisan boutiques and art galleries.

Geneva is also known for its watchmaking legacy, and horology lovers can visit several watch boutiques and museums. Watch enthusiasts should visit the Patek Philippe Museum and the Rolex Learning Centre.

Aside from traditional shopping experiences, Geneva has various department shops and shopping malls, such as Manor and Balexert, where tourists can buy a wide range of products, from fashion and cosmetics to electronics and home decor.

Overall, the shopping environment in Geneva is a mix of luxury, heritage, and diverse charm. Whether you're looking for high-end couture, unusual antiques, or a taste of Swiss workmanship, this cosmopolitan city provides a refined and diversified shopping experience.

Suggestions For Geneva Shopping

- **Rue du Rhône**: This is Geneva's principal retail street, and it is home to some of the world's most prestigious brands, including Gucci, Prada, and Louis Vuitton. Prices are suitably exorbitant, but you can expect the most recent designs and the highest quality.

- **Place du Molard**: Located in the centre of Old Town, this square is home to a variety of high-end stores as well as some more economical options. Everything from clothing and shoes to jewellery and watches may be found here.

- **Rue du Marché**: This street is famous for its classic Swiss stores, which sell everything from cheese and chocolate to cuckoo clocks and watches. Prices are lower here than on Rue du Rhône, and you're sure to find some one-of-a-kind gifts to take home.

- **The Old Town** is a fascinating network of narrow alleys and lanes filled with independent businesses selling everything from antiques and vintage apparel to art and crafts. This is an excellent location for finding one-of-a-kind gifts and souvenirs.

- **Shopping street in Old Town Geneva Confédération Centre**: This shopping mall in the city centre houses over 100 stores, including Zara, H&M, and Mango. Prices are lower here than on Rue du Rhône, and it's a terrific spot to shop for everyday products.

- **Bongénie Grieder says**: This department store is one of Geneva's oldest and most prominent, and it offers a wide range of high-end brands. Prices are exorbitant here, but you can expect top quality.

I hope this provides you some shopping ideas for Geneva. Have fun shopping!

Tips For Saving Money And Avoiding Tourist Traps

Do not purchase a tourist pass. These passes can be costly, and you may not be able to take advantage of all of the benefits. Instead, do some research to determine which attractions you want to visit and purchase tickets for each separately.

Avoid visiting the most popular tourist attractions. These locations are frequently busy and pricey. Explore the city's lesser-known areas instead, where you'll find more authentic experiences at lower pricing.

Make the most of free activities. Free activities in Geneva include visiting the Jet d'Eau, walking through the Old Town, and trekking up to the United Nations.

Eat at nearby establishments. Geneva has a diverse range of eateries, so you'll be able to find something to fit your budget. Avoid tourist traps and eat at restaurants frequented by locals.

Make use of public transit. Geneva has an excellent public transit system, so you won't need to rent a car to get around. You will save money on parking and gas as a result of this.

Here are a few particular ways you can save money in Geneva:

Take the normal train from Geneva Airport to the city centre instead of the City Airport Train. The regular train is CHF 6.60, while the City Airport Train is CHF 12.20.

Visit the Old Town instead of the International Red Cross and Red Crescent Museum. The Old Town is a UNESCO World Heritage Site that is free to visit.

Eat at a local eatery in one of the nearby neighbourhoods rather than a restaurant in Old Town. There will be better cuisine and lower prices.

Use public transportation instead of hiring a car. A single-day public transit pass costs CHF 8.20. You can save money while having a great time in Geneva if you follow these guidelines.

CHAPTER 7:RECOGNIZING FOREIGN TRANSACTION FEES

What do foreign transaction costs entail?

Credit card firms charge international transaction fees when you use your card to make a purchase in a foreign currency. These costs are usually a percentage of the purchase price plus a flat fee. A credit card firm, for example, may levy a 3% foreign transaction fee plus a $0.30 fixed cost.

How do I account for foreign transaction fees?

Foreign transaction fees are often presented as a separate charge on your credit card account. The cost will be referred to as a "foreign transaction fee" or a "FX fee." The fee amount will differ depending on your credit card company and the currency of the purchase.

What are the foreign transaction fees in Geneva?

Foreign transaction fees in Geneva vary based on your credit card company and the currency of purchase. However, as a general rule of thumb, overseas transaction fees should be roughly 3% of the purchase price. For example, if you spend CHF 100 ($100) in Geneva, you will pay approximately CHF 3 ($3) in foreign transaction costs.

How do I prevent paying foreign transaction fees?

When visiting Geneva, there are a few options for avoiding international transaction costs. One option is to use a credit card with no foreign transaction fees. There are other credit cards that provide this perk, so make sure to examine your alternatives before you travel.

Another approach to avoid foreign transaction fees is to use a debit card that does not charge them. Check with your bank, though, to determine if there are any penalties associated with using your debit card abroad.

Avoid Paying Cell Phone Roaming Fees.

What exactly are cell phone roaming charges? When you use your phone in a foreign nation, your cell phone provider will charge you roaming costs. These fees can be rather high, particularly for data usage. When you wander in Switzerland, one major cell phone carrier in the United States, for example, charges $0.25 per minute for voice calls, $0.20 each text message, and $10 per megabyte of data.

How can I prevent paying roaming charges in Geneva?

There are a few options for avoiding cell phone roaming charges in Geneva. One option is to disable your phone's data roaming capability. When you're in Switzerland, this will prevent your phone from connecting to the internet, but it will also prevent you from using any apps that require an internet connection.

Using a local SIM card is another approach to prevent cell phone roaming fees. Most convenience stores and electrical retailers in Geneva sell local SIM cards. You can use your phone to make calls, send text messages, and browse the internet after you have a local SIM card.

Map Download For Offline Use

Downloading maps for offline use has become a must-have feature for travelers, adventurers, and anyone navigating new terrain. Access to reliable maps without requiring an internet connection has been a game changer in an increasingly digital world. Having maps easily available offline provides piece of mind and ease when exploring distant areas, trekking through dense jungles, or just traveling to places with low network connection.

Users can access detailed and dynamic maps without an active internet connection by downloading maps onto a mobile device or GPS navigation system. Users can use this function to plan their trips, track their progress, and explore their surroundings even when internet access is limited or non-existent. Furthermore, offline maps frequently include extra features such as areas of interest, hiking trails, and local landmarks, which improves the entire navigating experience.

Offline map downloads have a number of advantages. They save money on data because they don't have to rely on a network connection all the time. They also ensure dependability because users may use maps whenever they choose, regardless of network availability. Furthermore, offline maps create a sense of security because visitors can rely on their downloaded maps even in an emergency or when unexpected circumstances develop.

Because of technology developments, many map programs and navigation systems now provide offline map downloads. Users may download specific regions or entire countries to their devices with a single tap, giving them access to comprehensive maps at any time and from any location.

Learn The Fundamentals Of The Language

Geneva has become a melting pot of languages from all over the world as the headquarters of various worldwide organisations, notably the United Nations and the Red Cross. However, one language is very important in the city: French, the official language of Geneva.

Learning the fundamentals of Geneva's language, French, opens you a world of opportunity for personal and professional development. The local populace speaks French, but it is also frequently used in international organisations, business settings, and academic institutions in Geneva. Learning French allows people to speak successfully with locals, make connections, and integrate into the community.

Furthermore, learning French gives you access to a plethora of cultural treasures. Geneva is famous for its thriving arts scene, which includes world-class museums, theatres, and music festivals. The works of prominent French-speaking authors, poets, and playwrights can be completely appreciated by learning French. Furthermore, French cuisine is revered in Geneva, and being able to read menus and communicate with local chefs enhances the dining experience.

Learning French also provides doors to a larger francophone world. French is spoken in many countries throughout the world, including Canada, Belgium, and several African countries. Learning French not only makes travel and cultural exploration easier, but it also improves career possibilities and opens up new markets for business potential.

The Cost Of Cash At The Airport Is High

The cost of cash at the airport is undeniably high, posing a significant inconvenience for travelers. While cash has long been a widely accepted form of payment, airports have gradually shifted towards a cashless environment due to various reasons, including efficiency, security, and operational streamlining.

One primary factor contributing to the high cost of cash at airports is the need for additional staffing and infrastructure. Handling cash transactions requires dedicated personnel, cash registers, and secure storage facilities, all of which incur expenses. Airports must invest in these resources, ultimately leading to higher operational costs that are often passed on to consumers.

Moreover, cash transactions typically involve more time and effort compared to electronic payments. Counting, verifying, and reconciling cash can lead to longer queues and delays, disrupting the overall flow of operations. As a result, airports may need to employ additional staff or extend their operating hours, further driving up costs.

Security concerns also play a significant role in the increasing unpopularity of cash at airports.

Handling large amounts of cash increases the risk of theft, both from external criminals and internal staff. To mitigate these risks, airports need to implement stringent security measures, including surveillance systems, security personnel, and specialized training, all of which contribute to the overall cost.

CONCLUSION

Travel Advice And Aditional Resourses

Finally, when it comes to travel advice, it is critical to consider the unique requirements and situations of various sorts of travelers, such as lone travelers, families, and LGBTQ people. While traveling to new places, each group may have different needs and confront different obstacles.

Prioritizing personal safety is critical for lone travelers. Researching the place ahead of time, exchanging travel plans with trusted individuals, and remaining cautious are all key measures. Taking advantage of local resources, such as tourist information centers or hotel concierge services, can provide essential direction and assistance throughout the voyage.

Families should prioritize preparing activities for all members and creating a child-friendly environment. It is critical to determine whether the destination has family-friendly accommodations, attractions, and services. Furthermore, keeping important documents, such as passports and medical information, immediately accessible is critical in case of an emergency.

It is critical for LGBTQ visitors to research the destination's cultural and legal context in terms of LGBTQ rights. Familiarizing oneself with local norms and legislation can assist in navigating potential obstacles. Connecting with LGBTQ travel communities, both online and in person, can provide useful information, recommendations, and support.

For all types of travelers, contact information and other tools are vital. Compiling a list of emergency contacts, including local authorities, embassies or consulates, and travel insurance providers, is vital prior to the journey. Additionally, using travel apps, online forums, and destination-specific guidebooks can provide useful information and recommendations.

Travelers can improve their safety, enjoyment, and overall experience by adapting travel guidance to the needs of lone travelers, families, and LGBTQ individuals. Adapting to the specific needs of each group promotes a more inclusive and fulfilling travel experience for all.

Directions from Geneva International Airport (GVA), Route de l'Aéroport, Grand-Saconnex, Switzerland to Cité Hostel Geneva, Rue Ferrier, Geneva, Switzerland

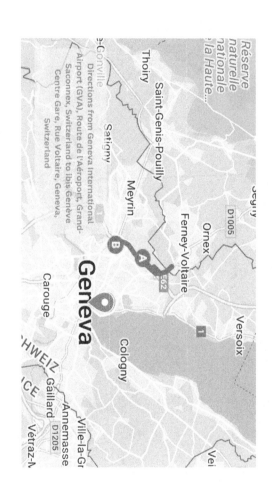

Directions from Geneva International Airport (GVA), Route de l'Aéroport, Grand-Saconnex, Switzerland to ibis Geneva Centre Gare, Rue Voltaire, Geneva, Switzerland

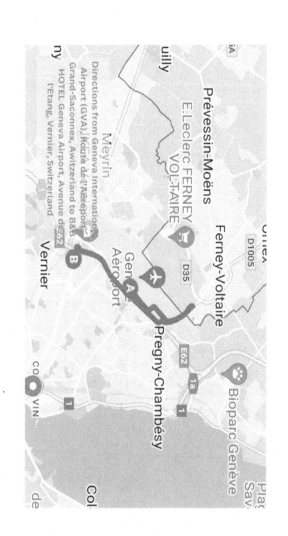

Directions from Geneva International Airport (GVA), Route de l'Aéroport, Grand-Saconnex, Awitzerland to B&B HOTEL Geneva Airport, Avenue de l'Etang, Vernier, Switzerland

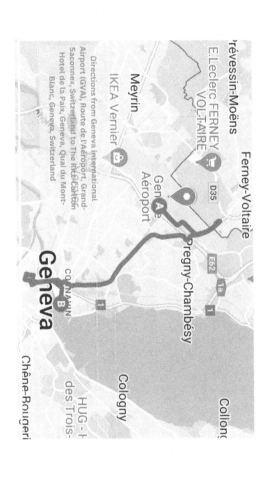

Directions from Geneva International Airport (GVA), Route de l'Aéroport, Grand-Saconnex, Switzerland to The Hotel - Hotel de la Paix, Geneva, Quai du Mont-Blanc, Geneva, Switzerland

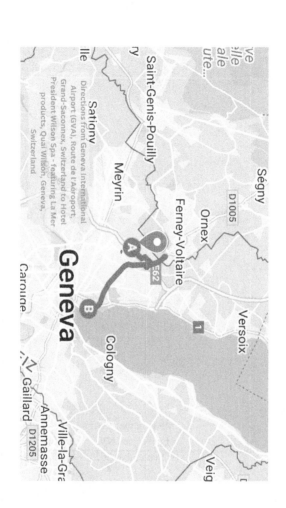

Directions from Geneva International Airport (GVA): Route de l'Aéroport, Grand-Saconnex, Switzerland to Hotel President Wilson Spa - Featuring La Mer products, Quai Wilson, Geneva, Switzerland

95

Made in the USA
Las Vegas, NV
03 September 2023